IRAN

CHINA

INDIA

THAILAND

AUSTRALIA

A Mealtime Manifesto

We think family mealtimes should be fun. There's a wealth of exciting dishes out there that the whole family can enjoy together.

This book is full of fascinating food facts from around the world, along with a recipe for each country we visit.

We don't expect kids to like everything they're given to eat. But we do believe if you tell them about the history and culture of food, it will inspire them to try something new.

We want to encourage the next generation to become inventive, passionate cooks, and leave them with a greater love and understanding of food.

AROUND THE WORLD WITH THE INGREEDIES

A Taste Adventure

Written by Zoë Bather and Joe Sharpe
Illustrated by Chris Dickason

LAURENCE KING PUBLISHING

CONTENTS

About the recipes

Our recipes are intended for families to cook together. Obviously older kids will need less help from an adult than younger ones. But there should always be adult supervision when cooking with heat, knives, or where any other potentially dangerous tasks are involved.

Each recipe has three main steps, and any bits the kids might like to get involved with are marked like this:

All of our recipes will feed four grown-ups, so you may want to adjust the portions slightly if your children are on the younger side.

Sometimes we've left stronger-tasting ingredients as optional, and generally seasoning is left to taste so that you can control the amount of salt you give them.

We always advocate buying free-range or organic meat (especially chicken and pork), and sustainably sourced seafood.

We also recommend keeping a well-stocked spice rack for adventurous mealtime travels!

Tuck in!

THE ADVENTURE BEGINS...

THE AMERICAS

Between the 15th and 20th centuries, the Americas were transformed by waves of European explorers and settlers, African slaves, and immigrants from all over the world.

As native populations mixed with new arrivals, a melting pot of different cultures evolved. We can see evidence of this in the food eaten across the nations of the Americas today.

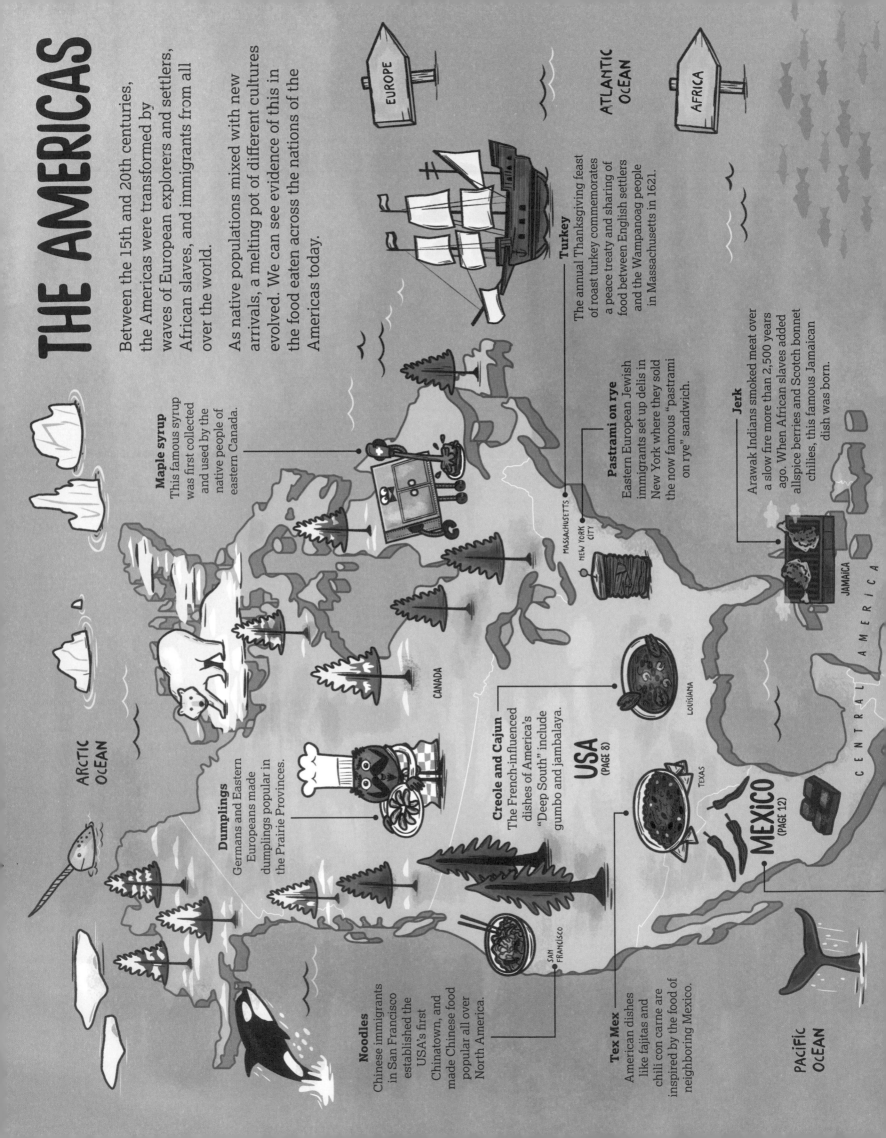

EUROPE

ATLANTIC OCEAN

AFRICA

Turkey
The annual Thanksgiving feast of roast turkey commemorates a peace treaty and sharing of food between English settlers and the Wampanoag people in Massachusetts in 1621.

Pastrami on rye
Eastern European Jewish immigrants set up delis in New York where they sold the now famous "pastrami on rye" sandwich.

Jerk
Arawak Indians smoked meat over a slow fire more than 2,500 years ago. When African slaves added allspice berries and Scotch bonnet chilies, this famous Jamaican dish was born.

Maple syrup
This famous syrup was first collected and used by the native people of eastern Canada.

Dumplings
Germans and Eastern Europeans made dumplings popular in the Prairie Provinces.

ARCTIC OCEAN

Noodles
Chinese immigrants in San Francisco established the USA's first Chinatown, and made Chinese food popular all over North America.

Creole and Cajun
The French-influenced dishes of America's "Deep South" include gumbo and jambalaya.

USA
(PAGE 8)

Tex Mex
American dishes like fajitas and chili con carne are inspired by the food of neighboring Mexico.

MEXICO
(PAGE 12)

PACIFIC OCEAN

MASSACHUSETTS

NEW YORK CITY

CANADA

LOUISIANA

TEXAS

SAN FRANCISCO

JAMAICA

CENTRAL AMERICA

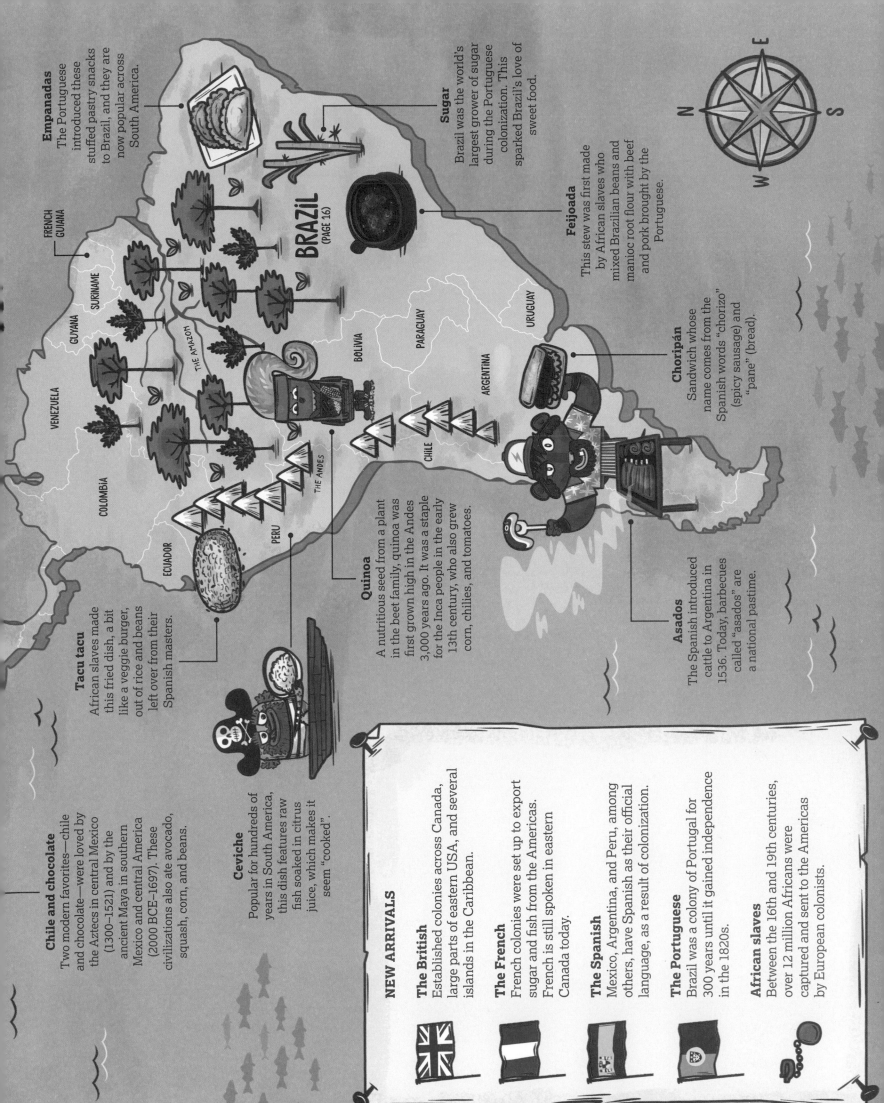

Empanadas
The Portuguese introduced these stuffed pastry snacks to Brazil, and they are now popular across South America.

Sugar
Brazil was the world's largest grower of sugar during the Portuguese colonization. This sparked Brazil's love of sweet food.

FRENCH GUIANA

SURINAME

GUYANA

BRAZIL (PAGE 16)

VENEZUELA

COLOMBIA

THE AMAZON

Feijoada
This stew was first made by African slaves who mixed Brazilian beans and manioc root flour with beef and pork brought by the Portuguese.

ECUADOR

PERU

THE ANDES

BOLIVIA

PARAGUAY

URUGUAY

CHILE

ARGENTINA

Choripán
Sandwich whose name comes from the Spanish words "chorizo" (spicy sausage) and "pane" (bread).

Quinoa
A nutritious seed from a plant in the beet family, quinoa was first grown high in the Andes 3,000 years ago. It was a staple for the Inca people in the early 13th century, who also grew corn, chilies, and tomatoes.

Asados
The Spanish introduced cattle to Argentina in 1536. Today, barbecues called "asados" are a national pastime.

Tacu tacu
African slaves made this fried dish, a bit like a veggie burger, out of rice and beans left over from their Spanish masters.

Ceviche
Popular for hundreds of years in South America, this dish features raw fish soaked in citrus juice, which makes it seem "cooked".

Chile and chocolate
Two modern favorites—chile and chocolate—were loved by the Aztecs in central Mexico (1300–1521) and by the ancient Maya in southern Mexico and central America (2000 BCE–1697). These civilizations also ate avocado, squash, corn, and beans.

NEW ARRIVALS

The British
Established colonies across Canada, large parts of eastern USA, and several islands in the Caribbean.

The French
French colonies were set up to export sugar and fish from the Americas. French is still spoken in eastern Canada today.

The Spanish
Mexico, Argentina, and Peru, among others, have Spanish as their official language, as a result of colonization.

The Portuguese
Brazil was a colony of Portugal for 300 years until it gained independence in the 1820s.

African slaves
Between the 16th and 19th centuries, over 12 million Africans were captured and sent to the Americas by European colonists.

U★S★A

The United States of America is a huge country made up of 50 individual states (one for each star on its flag). It stretches from the Arctic to the tropics and as far as Hawaii, in the middle of the Pacific Ocean.

The country has over two million farms, which produce delicious fruit, vegetables, and meat. Which job would you like to try? Harvesting corn in the Corn Belt, becoming a cowboy on a cattle ranch on the Great Plains, or picking some of the world's juiciest fruit in Florida and California?

BEEF PRIME CUTS
CHUCK
T-BONE
RIBEYE
BRISKET

Fruit
Farms in the USA grow lots of different types of fruit. It's cool in the north (perfect for blueberries) and steamy in the south (perfect for limes). It's all used to make amazing pies...

Florida Key lime pie
It's super-sharp!

Michigan cherry pie
With fab flaky pastry!

Maine blueberry pie
With lots of oozing juice!

IN SOME PARTS OF AMERICA, APPLE PIE IS SERVED WITH A WEDGE OF TANGY CHEDDAR CHEESE. YUMMY!

AMERICANS LOVE MILKSHAKES. THE LARGEST EVER MADE WAS IN NEW YORK AND WOULD HAVE FILLED A TANKER TRUCK.

The biggest ever pumpkin pie was made in Ohio. It was 20 feet wide and weighed as much as a small tractor.

Every November, Americans eat a roast turkey for Thanksgiving.

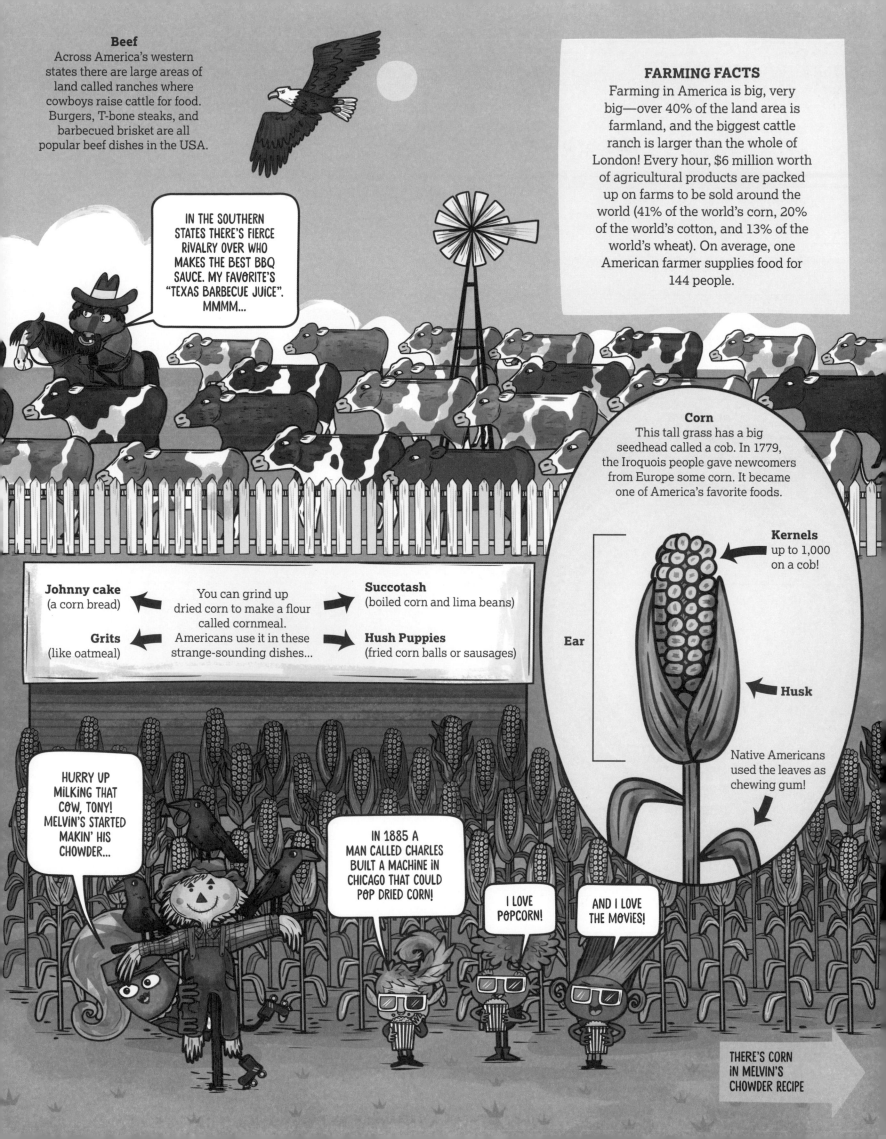

What is chowder?

New England, in the USA, is crazy about creamy, fishy chowder. In the 17th century, settlers sailed there from Europe and found a rocky coastline covered in clams. They used them to make a delicious soup. It's still made today, but it doesn't always have clams in it.

MELVIN'S AMERICAN
HADDOCK CHOWDER

SERVES 4

PREPARATION
10 minutes

COOKING
20 minutes

ESSENTIAL EQUIPMENT
Large pan with lid

INGREDIENTS
- **unsalted butter (4 tbsp)**
- **1 large white onion**, *peeled and finely chopped*
- **4 slices of smoked bacon**, *diced* (optional)
- **1 clove of garlic**, *peeled and chopped*
- **1 heaping tbsp all-purpose flour**
- **fish or vegetable bouillon (1¼ cups)**
- **semi-skim milk (1¼ cups)**
- **light cream (⅔ cup)**

- **1 bay leaf**
- **1 tsp dried thyme**
- **1 baking potato (approx. 9oz)**, *peeled and cut into small cubes*
- **canned corn kernels (1½ cups)**, *drained*
- **2 undyed smoked haddock fillets (about 14oz)**, *skin removed, cut into chunks (easiest done with scissors)*
- **3 tsp Dijon mustard**
- **juice of 1 lemon**

TO SERVE
- **fresh parsley**, *chopped*
- **crusty bread**

THANKS FOR THE CORN, LEXI!

STEP 1

Melt the butter in a large saucepan over medium heat.

STIR Stir in the onion. Then, after 2 minutes add the bacon and garlic.

Sweat the ingredients for another 3 minutes until they are soft but not colored, stirring gently and often.

Stir in the flour until completely mixed.

STEP 2

Stir in the bouillon, milk, and cream.

Then stir in the bay leaf, thyme, and potatoes.

SMELL Turn up the heat and bring to a boil, then reduce the heat and simmer for 12–15 minutes. Stir every so often so the sauce doesn't stick to the bottom of the pan. By now the potatoes should be nearly cooked; pierce them with a knife to check they're soft.

STEP 3

Add the corn and haddock to the soup and stir well. Put a lid on the pan.

Simmer for 5 minutes until the haddock is cooked through (the chunks will just be starting to break apart).

TASTE Stir in the Dijon mustard and lemon juice. Taste the liquid, and season with a little salt and pepper to taste.

This is great served with a sprinkling of chopped fresh parsley, and crusty bread.

MEXICO

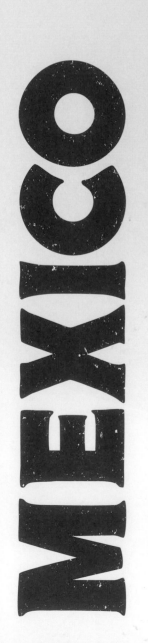

Wherever you are in Mexico, you'll never be far from a chile. Mexicans are mad for them. Essential for seasoning their eggs, beans, meat, and fish, chilies are so loved by the Mexicans that they even add them to their fruit salad!

Think you know your chilies? See how many you can recognize from our cheerful chile chart!

Cheerful chile chart

In 1912 Wilbur Scoville invented a scale to measure the heat level in chilies, which is known as the Scoville scale. Which of these have you tried?

🌶 = Scoville heat unit

1,569,000 🌶 Carolina Reaper (grown by a man called Ed Curriel)

1,463,000 🌶 Trinidad scorpion

1,100,000 🌶 Seven-pot habanero (each little pod can add fire to 7 pots of stew)

923,000 🌶 Dorset Naga

800,000–1,040,000 🌶 Bhut jolokia

Mexico's secret ingredient

The Maya made the world's first hot chocolate with chile and vanilla. Then the Aztecs became rich trading in chocolate. Today, Mexicans celebrate by eating "mole poblano" (turkey or chicken in a spicy chocolatey sauce).

It might sound weird putting chocolate into a savory dish, but it actually makes the sauce rich and smooth, NOT sweet or chocolatey.

LARRY'S MEXICAN
SPICY STREET WRAPS

SERVES 4

PREPARATION
10–15 minutes

COOKING
90 minutes

ESSENTIAL EQUIPMENT
A large, heavy-bottomed saucepan with a tight-fitting lid (you can use foil underneath the lid to make a tight seal)

INGREDIENTS
- ½ tsp chili powder
- 1 tbsp ground cumin
- 1 tbsp allspice
- 1 tsp smoked paprika
- 2 tsp dried oregano
- 1 tbsp sesame seeds
- **stewing beef (14oz)**, *diced*
- 1 tbsp olive oil
- **1 white onion**, *roughly chopped*
- **1 sweet red bell pepper**, *roughly chopped*
- **2 large cloves of garlic**, *peeled and crushed*
- **1 can of tomatoes (14oz)**, preferably plum, not chopped
- **dark chocolate (3 small squares)**

QUICK TOMATO SALSA
- **quarter of a small red onion**, *finely chopped*
- **3 ripe tomatoes**, *finely chopped*
- **handful of fresh cilantro**, *finely chopped*
- **dash of olive oil**
- **juice of 1 lime**

QUICK GUACAMOLE
- **1 large ripe avocado**, *roughly chopped*
- **quarter of a small red onion**, *finely chopped*
- **handful of fresh cilantro**, *finely chopped*
- **juice of half a lime**

TO SERVE
- **tortillas**, ideally corn but wheat is fine, *lightly toasted on each side in a dry skillet*
- **sour cream** (optional)

HOW MUCH CAN YOU FIT INSIDE YOUR TORTILLA?

STEP 1

Mix all the dry spices, oregano, and sesame seeds in a large bowl with a little salt and pepper. Add the beef to the bowl and mix thoroughly so that all the pieces are coated with the spice mix.

Heat the olive oil in the pan over medium heat. Add the onion and red pepper and fry them for 3 minutes until slightly soft.

SMELL Add the spiced beef and garlic, and fry, stirring continuously, until the meat is just seared all over (about 3 minutes).

Add the tomatoes and bring to a boil.

STEP 2

Turn down the heat, cover with a tight-fitting lid (or foil and a lid), and simmer over low heat for 60–90 minutes (the longer the better). Stir occasionally.

By now, the sauce should be nice and thick. If it's still a bit runny, turn up the heat and reduce the sauce with the lid off for another 10–15 minutes.

STIR Stir in the chocolate until melted.

Serve with the toasted tortillas (or some rice) along with sour cream, salsa, and guacamole.

STEP 3

QUICK TOMATO SALSA

Mix all the ingredients together in a bowl with a pinch of salt.

QUICK GUACAMOLE

 TASTE Mash the avocado in a bowl with a fork, and mix with the remaining ingredients and a good seasoning of salt.

Little stalls called "puestos" line Mexico's streets. They serve up snacks overflowing with colorful toppings of salsa, guacamole, cilantro, and cheese to passers-by.

BRAZIL

Brazil is the largest country in South America, and home to large parts of the Amazon rainforest and the River Amazon, the second longest river in the world. It winds its way from the Andes mountains in the west, to the Atlantic Ocean in the east.

The Amazon rainforest is a rich and diverse ecosystem. It's home to thousands of species of animals and plants, including lots of interesting things you can eat. Come and explore the undergrowth, and find some edible treats...

Brazil nuts
Crunch on some creamy nuts from the Brazil nut tree, which can live for 800 years.

Brazil nuts are actually seeds.

The shells are used as cups and are as big as coconuts.

Acai palm
Slurp a smoothie made from these blueberry-like berries. In Brazil you'll also find this "superfood" in sorbets, or served fresh with honey.

The tree is too tall to climb, so gatherers wait for the fruit to fall to the ground.

Guarana
Boost your energy levels with these seeds. They have twice the caffeine levels of coffee beans, so are used in "energy drinks". As the fruit ripens, it splits and a black seed emerges. Local people tell legends about this plant "of many eyes".

Fish
Tuck into some sun-dried fish, or maybe a "moqueca" (a stew of fish or shellfish, garlic, tomatoes, and coconut milk). If you ate a different Amazonian fish every day, it would take you years to try them all. Just watch out for those electric eels!!!

Surubim
Good for smoking, like salmon.

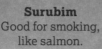

Piranha!

Pirarucu
One of the largest freshwater fish in the world, its flesh contains hardly any bones.

Pacu
Oily, small, and flat.

BENTLEY'S BRAZILIAN BRIGADEIROS

Said to be named after Brigadier Eduardo Gomes, these delicious little balls of yumminess are eaten all over Brazil, and are a celebration of one of the country's major exports: cocoa.

MAKES ABOUT 20 TRUFFLES

ESSENTIAL EQUIPMENT
- Heavy-bottomed saucepan
- Mini paper baking cups or waxed paper

INGREDIENTS
- butter (scant stick)
- condensed milk (approx. 14oz)
- 4 tbsp cocoa powder (good quality)
- chocolate sprinkles

Wipe the inside of a medium-sized bowl with butter.

Put a heavy-bottomed saucepan on low heat, and add the butter, then the condensed milk and cocoa powder. Stir the mixture constantly until the butter has melted, and the ingredients are combined.

Still stirring, turn up the heat and bring to a boil. Once boiling, turn the heat down to its lowest and continue to stir constantly for 10 minutes, making sure the mixture doesn't burn on the bottom. Transfer the mixture to the buttered bowl, and chill in the fridge for 2 hours so that you have a firm dough.

Butter your hands, then pinch off some of the dough to roll into small balls. Roll each ball in chocolate sprinkles, then put into mini baking cups or onto waxed paper.

Chocolate
Devour some chocolate, made from the beans of the cacao tree. This tree is happy living in the shade of taller plants, so you don't need to cut down the forest to grow it, which is good for the environment.

Bacuri fruit
Savor the amazing smell of this fruit. It's used to make ice creams, jellies, and juices.

Cashew nuts
Chomp on this ancient local snack, but you'll have to be quick—monkeys like this mild flavored nut as much as we do!

Pineapples
Pick a pineapple! They're part of the bromeliad family of plants that grow all over the rainforest. Their overlapping leaves catch rainwater, creating mini lakes for tiny frogs to live in.

Jambu leaves
Try a delicious duck stew made with this herb. It's also known as the "toothache plant" because it numbs your mouth!

Aviú
Tiny crustacean, eaten dried and salted.

Filhote
Means "little one".

Tambaqui
Tastes like pork.

Pescada amarela
Up to 3 feet long!

Electric eel!

EUROPE AND THE MEDITERRANEAN

Many European countries have a lot of coastline, making fish an important part of their diet. In northeastern areas such as Scandinavia and the Baltic, the Arctic air means that winters are bitterly cold. Oatmeal, desserts, and pancakes are popular for keeping the energy up.

Further south, warm sunshine around the Mediterranean Sea helps farmers grow citrus fruits, olives, and grapes, and raise cattle for making a range of delicious cheeses and other dairy products.

The North Sea
Fish grow more slowly and develop more flavor in cold water.

NORTH SEA

Moules-frites
Fresh mussels and fries are a Belgian favorite.

REPUBLIC OF IRELAND

UNITED KINGDOM

NETHERLANDS

BELGIUM

BRITISH ISLES
(PAGE 26)

Oysters
These saltwater clams thrive on the cool rocky coasts of Cornwall and Brittany.

Fondue
A big pot of hot melted cheese, popular with Alpine skiers. It's eaten with bread on a long fork.

FRANCE
(PAGE 20)

SWITZERLAND

N
W E
S

Gazpacho
A chilled soup for a hot day, made with sun-ripened tomatoes.

ATLANTIC OCEAN

PORTUGAL

SPAIN

Herbes de Provence
A blend of sun-loving marjoram, rosemary, oregano, and thyme.

Dates and apricots
These grow well in hot climates, and are cooked with meat in Morocco's famous tagines (a type of spicy stew).

Pimiento
These chilies are dried in the sun, ground and used in spicy paellas and chorizo sausage.

MEDITERRANEAN SEA

MOROCCO
(PAGE 36)

ALGERIA

TUNISIA

Couscous
Made from the durum wheat that grows here.

Harissa
Fiery red paste made from local Tunisian chilies.

18

Rømmegrøt
This cinnamon oatmeal will warm you up!

NORWAY

SWEDEN
(PAGE 30)

FINLAND

ESTONIA

DENMARK

LATVIA

Cloudberries
The plants these berries grow on can survive temperatures of -40°F.

RUSSIA

Mushrooms
These grow well in the cool forests of Russia.

Hunter's stew
The cabbage and apples used in this hearty stew grow well in the Lithuanian climate.

LITHUANIA

BELARUS

Blinis
Sun-shaped pancakes, eaten by early Europeans to bid farewell to winter.

GERMANY

Sauerkraut
Famous dish of cabbage, pickled for use in winter.

POLAND

UKRAINE

Dill
Popular herb grown in Eastern Europe. It's used in pickles, sour cream, and on potatoes.

Borscht
This steaming beet soup is said to have been invented in the Ukraine, where it's the national dish. Also popular in Poland, Lithuania, and Russia.

CZECH REPUBLIC

SLOVAKIA

AUSTRIA

HUNGARY

MOLDOVA

SLOVENIA

CROATIA

Poppies and sunflowers
These colorful crops are grown for their seeds and oil.

ITALY
(PAGE 32)

BOSNIA AND HERZEGOVINA

SERBIA

ROMANIA

Yogurt
The name of this cooling dairy product comes from Turkey, but it's used all over Europe, especially in the eastern Mediterranean.

BLACK SEA

MONTENEGRO

KOSOVO

ALBANIA

BULGARIA

MACEDONIA

Lemons
Grown on the sunny Amalfi coast. Perfect for a cooling sorbet.

GREECE

Mediterranean diet
People of the "Med" eat lots of fish, olive oil, fresh fruit, and vegetables, and are said to live longer as a result.

TURKEY

Baklava
Pistachio trees need hot, dry weather to produce the nuts used in this sweet Turkish pastry.

The French take their food very seriously. From the birth of "haute cuisine" to the development of restaurant culture, the French have always been a proud nation of food lovers.

Chef is busy in his French kitchen, where dishes are being prepared for hungry diners in the restaurant. Which job would you like to do?

Chop chop!
Auguste Escoffier was a famous French chef who invented the "brigade system", where all the cooks in the kitchen are given a particular job to do.

Season that sauce!
In classical French cuisine there are five "mother sauces". By adding other things to them you can make "daughter sauces". For example, Béchamel sauce becomes Mornay sauce by adding cheese.

Sauce Hollandaise
A base of butter, egg yolk, and lemon (for eggs or vegetables).

Sauce Béchamel
Milk-based sauce (for pasta, fish, or chicken).

Sauce Espagnole
Brown stock-based sauce (for poultry or meat).

Sauce velouté
White stock-based sauce (for fish or chicken).

Sauce tomate
Tomato-based sauce (for pasta, poultry, or meat).

Haute cuisine
"Haute cuisine" literally means "high cooking", and consists of rich, elaborately prepared, and beautifully presented meals containing lots of courses. What a treat!

> HMMM... I WONDER IF I WILL BE AWARDING THIS RESTAURANT ONE, TWO, OR THREE MICHELIN STARS?

CARTE (MENU)

HORS D'OEUVRES
(SNACKS BEFORE THE START OF THE MEAL)

ENTRÉE
(APPETIZER)

PLAT PRINCIPAL
(MAIN COURSE)

DESSERT
(DESSERT OF COURSE!)

FROMAGE
(CHEESE COURSE)

> BON APPETIT!

Look out, the Inspector is here!
Restaurant owners compete fiercely for Michelin stars. They were first awarded in 1926 by brothers André and Édouard Michelin (who made car tyres), in their famous restaurant guide for motorists.

Service!
The waiter's job is very important in the restaurant. As well as serving the food, waiters are also expected to have an excellent knowledge of the recipes and ingredients used.

> WHO CAN NAME SOME FAMOUS FRENCH DISHES?

> MAYONNAISE!!! I PUT IT ON EVERYTHING!

> SOUFFLÉS AND OMELETS! THEY'RE THE BEST

A funny mouthful
"Amuse-bouche" means "mouth-amuser"! It's a bite-sized gift from the chef, to awaken your tastebuds before your meal arrives. It's often served on a spoon.

France OUT AND ABOUT

As well as its celebrated restaurants and recipes, France is also world-famous for the bread, meat, pâtés, cheeses, and pastries it produces.

In every French town you'll find a boulangerie for your bread, a charcuterie for your sausages, a fromagerie for your cheese, and a pâtisserie for your cakes. What would you buy for your perfect French picnic?

THE WORD "CROISSANT" COMES FROM THE FRENCH FOR "CRESCENT"

Eclairs
Don't forget your chocolate éclair! Made from a light pastry and filled with cream, an éclair is the ultimate sweet treat. Which flavored cream are you having: vanilla, coffee, or chocolate?

BOULANGERIE

CHARCUTERIE

Patisserie

SAUCISSON JAMBON

PÂTÉ TERRINE

BRIOCHE

PAIN AU CHOCOLAT

CROISSANT

I HOPE BENTLEY'S GETTING MY PEARS

HEY, RITA!

OUVERT DÈS 6H

TARTE TATIN

TARTE AUX FRUITS

ÉCLAIR

Baguette
Nothing is more French than bread, and the baguette is essential to any picnic. Some say the French emperor Napoleon asked for his bread to be made long and thin so his soldiers could carry it down their pants. And voilà, the baguette was invented!

Saucisson
Meat products like bacon, ham, sausages, terrines, and pâtés are known as "charcuterie" in France. The saucisson (a thick sausage) is a particularly popular purchase. This salted and dried snack came about as a way of preserving meat before the fridge was invented. Nowadays it's the perfect portable treat to pop in your picnic basket.

HOW TO MAKE CHEESE

1
Add some special cheese bacteria and some rennet (an enzyme from the stomach of a calf) to fresh whole milk.

2
The milk will separate into curds (solid bits) and whey (the leftover watery bits). Drain the whey from the curds.

3
Put the curds in a mold and press them.

4
Wrap the cheese in cloth and leave it to mature (develop its flavor).

Fruit and vegetables
Crudités (sliced raw vegetables) are perfect for a picnic. Try dipping them in a French vinaigrette (a salad dressing of olive oil, vinegar, and herbs). As the seasons pass, French fruit bowls are filled with the ripest of raspberries, sweetest of strawberries, and reddest of red currants...

CASSIS
POMMES
FRAMBOISES
CERISES
FRAISES
PÊCHES
PRUNES
POIRES

FROMAGERIE

POISSONNERIE

Epicerie

ROQUEFORT
CHÈVRE
CAMEMBERT
COMTÉ

HUÎTRES   MOULES

ARE YOU BRAVE ENOUGH TO TRY ONE OF THESE LITTLE NIPPERS?

THESE APPLES WILL BE PERFECT FOR PUTTING IN RITA'S TART!

DID YOU GET THE PEARS, BENTLEY?

I HOPE HE DIDN'T GET APPLES AGAIN!

Cheese
The French have a saying that "a meal without cheese is like a day without sunshine". With over 500 types to try, you could be eating a different cheese every day of the year! In a trip to the fromagerie you'll find small balls, long cylinders, pyramids, gigantic wheels, or even heart-shaped varieties. And the cheeses don't just taste cheesy— they can be sweet, nutty, earthy, salty, acidic, or even metallic!

Oysters
These slippery little sea creatures are eaten straight from the shell, usually with a little lemon juice. The French poet Léon-Paul Fargue said eating oysters was "like kissing the sea on the lips".

TARTE TATIN CAN BE MADE WITH PEARS OR APPLES

The great tarte Tatin

The tarte Tatin was named after two sisters, Stéphanie and Caroline Tatin. Legend has it that Stéphanie was making an apple pie for the guests at her hotel, but her apples started to burn in the sugary butter. To rescue the dish, she quickly put the pastry on top of the apples and put it in the oven upside down. The tart was greedily devoured by her guests, and the hotel became famous for this unusual but delicious dish.

PEAR TARTE TATIN

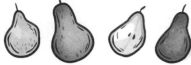

SERVES 4

PREPARATION
10 minutes

COOKING
45 minutes

ESSENTIAL EQUIPMENT
• An ovenproof skillet, approx. 10 inches in diameter
• Oven gloves
• Serving plate

INGREDIENTS
• **unsalted butter (4 tbsp)**, *cut into small cubes*
• **superfine sugar (¾ cup)**
• **6 Anjou pears** (other varieties of pear or apples also work well) *peeled, cored and cut into quarters*
• **puff pastry (12oz sheet)**, *at room temperature*
• **flour**, for dusting

TO SERVE
• **Great with crème fraîche or a scoop of vanilla ice cream**

> PEOPLE ALSO MAKE THIS TART WITH PEACHES, PINEAPPLE, OR BANANAS.

STEP 1

Preheat the oven to 425°F (400°F fan)

MELT Heat your ovenproof skillet on the stovetop, over medium low heat. Melt the butter in the pan and sprinkle over the sugar evenly to make the caramel. Do not stir. Leave for around 5 minutes until the sugar has dissolved, and the mixture starts to darken.

Arrange the pear quarters in a circle around the edge of the caramel mixture, filling the center with the last few pieces. Turn up the heat slightly so the caramel starts to gently bubble, but still no stirring! The pears should take about 20–30 minutes to cook. To test when they're ready, prick with a sharp knife—they should be nice and soft.

STEP 2

CUT Meanwhile, dust a clean work surface with flour, lay out the pastry, and cut out a circle slightly larger than the size of the skillet.

Once the pears have cooked and softened, turn the heat off and place the pastry over the pears. Tuck the pastry in around the edge of the pan with a wooden spoon, and prick the surface with a fork to create holes for the steam to escape.

Bake in the oven for 15 minutes, until the pastry is cooked and golden.

STEP 3

Using oven gloves, carefully remove **BASH** the pan from the oven. If the center of the pastry has risen to form a mound, bash it carefully with a rolling pin to flatten (this will help prevent the pears falling into the center when you turn it). Leave for 5 minutes to cool.

When turning the tart, always use oven gloves as the pan handle and caramel will still be very hot. Carefully place a serving plate over the pan, and quickly flip the pan over, so the tart sits on the plate, pear side up.

Serve with crème fraîche or vanilla ice cream.

CAREFUL!
Turning the tarte Tatin is definitely NOT a job for the kids to try. Be extra careful and always use oven gloves.

The British Isles

The British Isles have been disconnected from mainland Europe since the end of the last Ice Age. Local food and eccentric traditions can be found all across the nations of the British Isles, wherever you go and whatever time of year! Find out what's happening this month with our Calendar of Curiosities.

Cullen skink
A delicious creamy soup of smoked fish and potatoes.

Haggis
A famous Scottish delicacy of oats, spices, and offal (heart, lungs, and liver), boiled in a sheep's stomach.

SCOTLAND

Arbroath smokies
Haddock rubbed in salt and smoked in a barrel.

Soda bread
A cross cut in the top of the bread was thought to protect the household from the Devil.

NORTHERN IRELAND

Yorkshire pudding
This fluffy batter made from eggs, flour, and milk goes with your roast dinner. Long ago, it used to be eaten before the meat (which was expensive) to fill you up.

Kendal Mint Cake
Sir Edmund Hillary ate this sugary, peppermint-flavored bar on top of Mount Everest.

REPUBLIC OF IRELAND

Lincolnshire sausage
Romans in this area put sage in their sausages so they stayed fresh for longer.

Colcannon
An old Irish tradition is to hide a prize (often money) inside this dish of mashed potatoes and cabbage.

Laverbread
Made from boiled and mashed laver, a type of seaweed.

Welsh rarebit
A mixture of cheese, mustard, and beer, spread on toast and broiled.

WALES

ENGLAND

Cromer crab
Served whole with samphire, a salty coastal vegetable.

Cornish pasty
Traditionally eaten by tin miners in Cornwall, pasties often had two courses inside (meat, swede, and potato in one end, and jam in the other!).

Stargazy pie
A fish pie with a pastry lid, with the heads of the fish sticking up through it toward the sky.

Cheddar cheese
First made, and left to mature, in caves near the village of Cheddar, this is now the most popular cheese in Britain.

Jellied eels
Popular in the pie and mash shops of East London, this is a dish of boiled eels, set in their own jelly. It's eaten cold.

CALENDAR OF CURIOSITIES

THE HERBS' PIE USES TWO TYPES OF ENGLISH CHEESE...

BURNS NIGHT

JANUARY

Scottish poet Robert Burns loved haggis so much he wrote a poem about it. Now people celebrate his birthday by eating it!

COLLOP MONDAY

FEBRUARY

On the day before Shrove Tuesday (pancake day), fried bacon (collops) and eggs were traditionally eaten. Children in Yorkshire, Lancashire, and Durham used to go from door to door singing "Today is Collop Monday, gie's a collop, an' let's away".

MOTHER'S DAY

MARCH

Traditional treats to give your mom included mothering buns in Bristol, simnel cake in Bury, and fig pie in Blackburn.

ST MARK'S EVE

APRIL

On the eve of the feast of St Mark, unmarried women would bake "dumb cake" to conjure up a dream that would reveal who their future husband would be. The cake was made in complete silence.

SHHHHHH!

CHEESE ROLLING

MAY

Every Spring Bank Holiday, a large Double Gloucester cheese is rolled down Cooper's Hill near Gloucester, with competitors racing after it. The cheese can reach speeds of 70 mph.

EGG THROWING

JUNE

The village of Swaton hosts the World Egg Throwing Championships, where couples throw raw eggs to each other. The team to throw the farthest distance without breaking or dropping the egg wins the trophy.

OYSTER FESTIVAL

JULY

Known for its oysters since Norman times, Whitstable has a festival that begins with the landing of the oysters (the first catch of the season). There's an oyster-eating competition at the harbor—the person to eat six oysters in the fastest time wins!

FEAST OF ST OSWALD

AUGUST

In the 1800s, people bringing rushes to cover the earth floor of Grasmere Church were given gingerbread as payment. Nowadays, this snack is eaten on special occasions such as the Feast of St Oswald.

BLACK PUDDING THROWING

SEPTEMBER

It's said that during the "Wars of the Roses" between the Houses of Lancaster and York, each side threw food at each other when their ammunition ran out. This ancient grudge is re-enacted every September by hurling Lancashire black puddings at a pile of Yorkshire puddings.

PUNKIE NIGHT

OCTOBER

In Somerset, children would march the streets with a pumpkin lantern singing:

"It's Punkie Night tonight
It's Punkie Night tonight
Adam and Eve would not believe
It's Punkie Night tonight."

SWAN FEAST

NOVEMBER

Cooked like a chicken, swans were a medieval delicacy. They were eaten stuffed with herbs at the annual Swan Feast. The celebration still exists, but swan is no longer eaten as apparently it tastes horrible.

TOM BAWCOCK'S EVE

DECEMBER

Stargazy pie is eaten in Mousehole in Cornwall on 23 December, in memory of a legendary fisherman who is said to have saved the village from starvation by battling a terrifying storm to bring home a bumper catch of fish.

Pie fanatics

There are as many types of pie on these isles as there are weeks of the year. Meat, fish, or veg? Shortcrust, flaky, or puff pastry? Hot or cold? Big or small? The choice is endless.

There's even a pie for weddings! Hidden inside the traditional "Bride's Pie" was a glass ring. Whoever found the ring, according to the custom, would be the next to marry.

CHEESY CHIVY PIE

SERVES 4

PREPARATION
20 minutes

COOKING
1 hour

ESSENTIAL EQUIPMENT
- A pie pan, approx. 9in round and 2in deep, ideally made of metal
- Rolling pin

PIE
- **unsalted butter (2 tbsp)** (plus extra for greasing)
- **2 large red onions (approx. 14oz)**, *sliced into rings*
- **1 tsp English mustard**, *mixed with one-third of a cup of water*
- **1 pack of shortcrust pastry (18oz)**, at room temperature
- **Lancashire cheese (1½ packed cups)**, *grated*
- **strong Cheddar cheese (1 packed cup)**, *grated*
- **fresh chives (¼ cup)**, *chopped*
- **black pepper**

SALAD
- **mixed salad leaves**
- **half a cucumber**, *halved lengthwise and sliced*
- **1 crunchy red apple**, *cored and thinly sliced*
- **1 tbsp olive oil**
- **1 tbsp cider vinegar**
- **1 tsp wholegrain mustard**
- **½ tsp honey**
- **fresh chives**, *chopped*

> CHIVES ARE THE PERFECT PARTNER FOR CHEESE

STEP 1

Preheat the oven to 400°F (350°F fan)

MELT Melt the butter in the saucepan over medium heat.

Add the sliced onions and cook for 10–15 minutes, stirring occasionally so they don't burn. The onions should be nearly soft, but with a slight bite.

Stir in the water and mustard mixture and cook for another 2 minutes. Tip the onions into a large mixing bowl and allow to cool a little.

Grease the inside of the pie pan with a little butter.

STEP 2

ROLL On a floured surface, roll out two-thirds of the pastry to ⅛ inch thickness.

Place the rolled pastry in the pie pan (so it covers the bottom and sides), and press the pastry into the pan's corners if necessary.

Add the grated cheeses and chopped chives to the cooled onion. Season generously with black pepper and mix well. Tip the mixture into the pie pan and level it out with a spoon.

Moisten the pastry on the rim of the pie pan with a little water.

STEP 3

CRIMP Roll out the remaining pastry. Cut it to just larger than the pie pan and lay it over the pie filling. Using the back of a fork, press the pastry lid down into the pastry below it, crimping the edges to seal.

Run a knife around the edge of the dish to trim off any excess pastry. Make a couple of slits in the pastry lid with a knife (so that the steam can escape). Cook the pie in the oven for about 45 minutes, until the pastry is golden brown.

Remove from the oven and allow the pie to cool. It can be eaten hot, but is best served at room temperature.

While the pie is cooling, make your salad dressing by mixing the olive oil, cider vinegar, wholegrain mustard, honey, and chives in a small cup. Mix the salad leaves, cucumber, and apple in a bowl. Pour over the dressing just before you're ready to eat.

> JUST LIKE TARRAGON AND CHICKEN...

> ...OR FISH AND PARSLEY!

SWEDEN

Since prehistoric times (long before the fridge was invented), humans have been finding ways to store food gathered in summer, so that it can be eaten in winter when fresh ingredients are scarce.

In Sweden, where winters are long and very cold, preserving food has always been an important tradition. The Ingreedies are trying their hand at a few preserving techniques. Why not have a go at pickling some cucumber for a "smörgås"?

Crackers about crackers
Crispbread ("knäckebröd") has been made in Sweden since AD 500. This light and crunchy snack, made with rye flour, was traditionally baked just twice a year, as it keeps fresh for a very long time.

CRISPBREADS HAD HOLES iN THE MiDDLE SO THEY COULD BE STORED ON STiCKS OVER THE WiNTER

Smitten with smoking
Smoking not only preserves food, but also adds flavor. Wood smoke kills bacteria and seals the food from the air, making it last much longer. Bacon and mackerel taste really good smoked.

DiD YOU KNOW THAT DiFFERENT TYPES OF WOOD CREATE DiFFERENT FLAVORED SMOKES?

I MUST GET SOME BLUEBERRY SOUP READY FOR THE SKi MARATHON!

Bonkers for berries
In the summer, berries are picked from the forests and fields and made into jams and soups—so you can have a taste of summer sun in the chilliest winter months.

Cloudberries

Elderberries

Blueberries

Medieval Swedish fishermen preserved fish by burying it in the ground. They called it "surfisk".

One way to preserve fish for the winter is to dry it. "Lutefisk" is dried cod, traditionally eaten on Christmas Eve.

Wild strawberries

Lingonberries

Rowan berries

30

THE HERBS' SWEDISH SMÖRGÅS

Smörgås are Swedish open sandwiches, and are usually part of a "smörgåsbord" (a buffet of hot and cold dishes). Try making this delicious cucumber pickle for your own smörgås.

MAKES ENOUGH PICKLE FOR 6–8 SMÖRGÅS

CUCUMBER PICKLE
- **one third of a cucumber**, *very thinly sliced*
- **2 tsp salt**
- **2 tbsp white wine vinegar**
- **¼ tsp white pepper**
- **½ tsp mustard seeds**
- **1 tsp superfine sugar**
- **2 tsp fresh dill** (optional), *finely chopped*

TO SERVE
- **smoked fish**, *mashed into a paste with a fork* (mackerel or herring is good)
- **hard or blue cheese**
- **toasted rye bread or crackers**

Mix the cucumber thoroughly with the salt in a bowl, then leave for 10 minutes.

Mix the vinegar, pepper, mustard seeds, sugar, and dill in another bowl.

After 10 minutes in the salt, rinse the cucumber really thoroughly to remove all the salt, then squeeze out any excess water with your hands.

Mix with the vinegar mixture and leave for another 10 minutes, then your pickle is ready.

To assemble your smörgås, put the fish or cheese on the bread or crackers, and top with the pickle.

Dotty for dill
Dill is an herb that tastes like a mixture of fennel, aniseed, and celery. Its feathery leaves are scattered on fish or potatoes, stirred into sauces, or mixed with vinegar and used to pickle cucumbers.

Rollmops are herring rolled around cucumber, onion or another filling, and pickled in vinegar.

Stinky surströmming
This canned herring, fermented in salt, is an acquired taste. It's one of the smelliest foods in the world, so it's usually eaten outdoors!

Herring swim in enormous shoals. They are often eaten smoked or broiled.

CAN YOU GUYS PICKLE ME SOME CUCUMBER FOR MY SMÖRGÅS?

WHAT SHALL WE PUT IN THE PICKLE?

ERR, HOW ABOUT DILL?

NO! MUSTARD SEEDS!

I DO LOVE ROLLMOPS!

WHO PUT THAT THERE?!!!

31

ITALY

Food is at the heart of the Italian family. Secret recipes for the tastiest tomato sauce or perfect pasta have been passed down from generation to generation.

Tony's mama is the boss of this kitchen, and she has everyone pitching in to help! If you get invited to dinner in Italy, remember to wipe your plate with some bread – this shows how much you enjoyed it.

THE ROMANS MADE A SAUCE WITH ANCHOVIES CALLED GARUM. ANCHOVIES GIVE A SALTY, YUMMY KICK TO YOUR TOMATO SAUCE...

I HOPE THIS MEAL HAS 10 COURSES LIKE LAST TIME!

WITH OVER 200 TYPES OF PASTA TO TRY, WHICH SHOULD I CHOOSE?

TONY'S MAMA

IT'S ALL IN THE SHAPE, CHAI. LIGHT SAUCES GO WITH LONG PASTA. THICKER SAUCES GO WITH PASTA SHAPES. REALLY THICK SAUCES GO WITH PASTA TUBES.

PASTA
This starchy, savory dish is eaten almost every day by Italians.

Pasta secca (dried pasta)

Flour   Water

Pasta fresca (fresh pasta)

Flour   Eggs

PASTA SHAPES

Farfalle (means "butterfly")

Conchiglie (means "shell")

Orecchiette (means "little ear")

PASTA TUBES

Penne

Rigatoni (means "lined")

Macaroni

LONG PASTA

Spaghetti   Tagliatelle   Pappardelle

The world record for the longest strand of pasta is 4,122 yards!

Colored pasta is made using spinach or tomato. You can even flavor your pasta with squid ink or chocolate!

Ravioli are mini "sandwiches" made of two flat squares of pasta with a meat or vegetable filling.

Olive oil

Olives

The fruit of the olive tree is essential in Italian cooking. Olives are stored in jars for eating as part of "antipasti" (a type of appetizer) with ham and sun-dried tomatoes. They are also pressed and turned into olive oil, which is used for cooking and dressing salads. As olives ripen, they turn from green to black. Black olives are softer and less bitter than green ones.

Olive tree
Can live for hundreds of years.

Basil

I MUST GET THE RECIPE FOR MAMA'S TOMATO SAUCE... IT SMELLS DELICIOUS!

THE ROMANS LOVED OLIVES. THEY ATE THEM BLINDFOLDED AND TRIED TO GUESS WHERE THEY HAD BEEN GROWN.

I HEARD THEY BELIEVED IF YOU LEFT A BASIL LEAF UNDER A POT IT WOULD TURN INTO A SCORPION!

MMMM, PASTA COOKED "AL DENTE" (FIRM TO THE BITE)

Basil
This sun-loving herb is a tomato's best friend. It's also delicious with capers, zucchini, and mozzarella. Basil is best used raw or at the end of cooking to preserve its flavor. Try growing some in a pot on a sunny windowsill.

Parmesan
This sweet, nutty, salty cheese is great on pasta. Astronauts eat lots of parmesan as it's full of calcium that keeps their bones strong.

Garlic
This little bulb, which is related to the onion, is packed with a pungent flavor, perfect for pairing with pasta. The Romans believed that garlic gave you strength and courage, so they fed it to their soldiers.

Pesto
This thick paste of basil, olive oil, pine nuts, and garlic is amazing stirred through pasta. Try making your own pestos by using different herbs and nuts (marjoram, sage, walnuts, and hazelnuts all work well).

Ciabatta
great for sandwiches

Focaccia
softer and sweeter

BREAD

Pane alle olive
with olives

Taralli Pugliesi
crunchy bread rings

Balsamic vinegar
This sweet, dark vinegar is perfect for dressing salad or dunking pieces of bread in. A dash in your tomato sauce will make it the best ever...

TASTE TONY'S TERRIFIC TOMATO SAUCE FOR PIZZA!

The Queen of Pizzas

The Margherita pizza (bottom right) is said to have been named after Italy's Queen Margherita in 1889. The tomato, mozzarella and basil symbolize the three colors of the Italian flag.

TONY'S ITALIAN
PiZZA PiCKS

MAKES 2 LARGE PIZZAS WITH 3 TOPPING CHOICES

PREPARATION
- Dough: 10 minutes
  (+ 1 hour resting)
- Sauce: 5 minutes
- Toppings: 10 minutes

COOKING
- Sauce: 40 minutes
- Pizza: 15 minutes

ESSENTIAL EQUIPMENT
- Rolling pin
- 2 pizza stones
  (or upturned baking trays)

2 LARGE PIZZA BASES
- **strong bread flour (1⅔ cups)**
- **1 envelope (2¼ tsp) of active dried yeast**
- **warm water (⅔ cup)**
- **2 tbsp olive oil**

TOMATO SAUCE FOR 2 PIZZAS
- **2 tbsp olive oil**
- **1 medium white onion**, *finely chopped*
- **2 large cloves of garlic**, *peeled and crushed*
- **1 can of good-quality plum tomatoes (14oz)**
- **2 tsp balsamic vinegar**
- **½ tsp salt**
- **black pepper**

MARGHERITA TOPPING FOR 1 PIZZA
- **mozzarella (3oz)**, *roughly chopped*
- **a handful of fresh basil leaves**

FIORENTINA TOPPING FOR 1 PIZZA
- **spinach (approx. 4oz)**, *wilted in a dry non-stick pan with a lid on*
- **mozzarella (3oz)**, *roughly chopped*
- **1 egg**
- **a sprinkling of grated nutmeg**
- **a sprinkling of parmesan**, *grated*

NAPOLETANA TOPPING FOR 1 PIZZA
- **mozzarella (3oz)**, *roughly chopped*
- **8 anchovies** (jarred or canned)
- **2 tsp capers**
- **1 tsp dried oregano**

THE FiORENTiNA IS MY FAVOURITE!

STEP 1

THE PIZZA BASES
Mix the flour and yeast in a large bowl. Make a well in the flour and pour the warm water and oil into it. Mix to form a soft dough, then place on a clean, floured work surface.

KNEAD Knead the dough for 5 minutes until it becomes elastic in texture. Then shape it into a large ball and place it in a clean bowl covered with a clean dish towel. Leave in a warm place for about an hour until it has roughly doubled in size.

STEP 2

THE TOMATO SAUCE
Warm 1 tablespoon of the oil in a medium, nonstick saucepan, add the onion and gently cook on low heat for 7 minutes, stirring regularly, until soft but not colored. Add the garlic and continue to cook for 3 minutes.

STIR Stir in the tomatoes, balsamic, salt, and a sprinkling of black pepper. Break up the tomatoes a bit with the back of a wooden spoon. Bring to a boil, then simmer on low heat for 30 minutes, stirring often.

By now, the sauce should be nice and thick. Take off the heat and stir in the remaining tablespoon of olive oil.

STEP 3

Preheat the oven to 400°F (350°F fan)

TOPPINGS AND COOKING
Divide the dough into 2 balls and roll out each one to make a disk about ¼ inch thick. Place each pizza base on a pizza stone (or large upturned baking pan greased with butter), then cover with 2 tablespoons of the tomato sauce.

TOP Arrange the toppings in the order they appear in the ingredients list. For the Fiorentina, carefully crack an egg onto the pizza and sprinkle over the nutmeg and parmesan before putting in the oven.

Cook each pizza for 15 minutes.

Morocco

Morocco is one of the most diverse countries in Africa, with coastal plains, high mountains, parched desert, and bustling cities full of ancient, winding alleys.

There's no better place to sample the delights of Moroccan food than in a "souq". A dazzling array of ingredients can be found in these famous street markets. So take a deep breath, and savor the many sounds, sights, and smells of the souq!

Tagines
Tagines are a popular stew in Morocco. They are named after the tall earthenware pot they're cooked in.

Couscous
These tiny balls of wheat are eaten throughout North Africa. To make couscous, you mix flour and salty water, then rake it through with your fingers, before leaving it to dry.

NOW WHAT WAS IT CHEF WANTED ME TO GET...

...WAS IT COUSCOUS?

THOSE SPICES SMELL AMAZING, LEXI

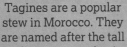

COUSCOUS

CARDAMOM

GINGER

TURMERIC

CLOVES

CINNAMON

NUTMEG

Spices
Eastern spices like cinnamon were brought to Morocco by the Arab invaders in the seventh century. "Ras-el-hanout" is a blend of a shop's best spices. It's used to sprinkle over dishes or rub into meat.

Floral water
Made in spring from rose petals, it takes months for the flavor of rosewater to develop. It's used in Moroccan jams, drinks, and pastries.

Dates
There are over 30 different types of date palm tree. They produce a nutritious, sugary fruit. Some dates are so sweet you can see syrup dripping from them on the tree!

PLUMS

Fruit
Fruit is a big part of the Moroccan diet. It might be added to a lamb or chicken tagine, or eaten raw as a refreshing end to the meal.

OLIVES

DATES

PEACHES

GRAPES

MELONS

HONEY

Sweetness
Mixing sweet and savory flavors defines the taste of Morocco. The sweetness often comes from dried fruit like apricots, or honey.

APRICOTS

SEE WHAT CHEF DOES WITH ALL THESE AMAZING INGREDIENTS...

Citrus fruit
Citrus fruit grow all year round in Morocco because the weather is warm. Jewish Moroccans are said to have developed the art of preserving lemons, which are used in lots of Moroccan dishes.

GRAPEFRUITS

ORANGES

LEMONS

BASTILLA

ALMONDS

One sweet layer of almonds, confectioners' sugar and cinnamon

Two savory layers of ras-el-hanout and pigeon

Almonds
Almonds are used a lot in Moroccan cooking. Especially in "bastilla", a sweet and savory pie made with layers of paper-thin pastry called "warqa", which means "leaf".

Mint tea
Mint tea is often served with an almond pastry called "qa'b el-ghazal".

The tagine

Moroccan stews are often made in tagines. They were the pot of choice for the nomadic Berber people who could carry them on their travels across the desert. A fire would be lit in a matching pan called a "majmar" which sat below the tagine—perhaps one of the first camping stoves!

CHEF'S MOROCCAN
CHICKEN STEW

SERVES 4

PREPARATION
15 minutes

COOKING
1 hour

ESSENTIAL EQUIPMENT
A large, wide, heavy-bottomed pot or pan, with a tight-fitting lid (you can use foil underneath the lid to make a tight seal)

INGREDIENTS
- **2 tbsp olive oil**
- **1 large white onion**, *peeled and thinly sliced*
- **3 cloves of garlic**, *peeled and finely sliced*
- **1 tsp ground ginger**
- **1 tsp ground turmeric**
- **1 tsp ground black pepper**
- **1 cinnamon stick**, or ½ tsp of ground cinnamon
- **1 bunch fresh parsley**, *stalks and leaves separated and chopped*
- **zest and juice of 1 lemon**
- **4 large skinless chicken thighs** (free-range or organic if possible)
- **1 large carrot**, *sliced*
- **1 large zucchini**, *halved and sliced*
- **dried apricots (⅓ cup)**, *halved*
- **1 tbsp honey**

TO SERVE
- **slivered almonds (⅔ cup)**, *lightly toasted in a dry skillet*
- **Israeli couscous** (ordinary couscous or rice is also nice)

> MY STEW HAS ALL THE FLAVORS OF A MOROCCAN TAGINE, BUT YOU DON'T NEED A SPECIAL POT TO MAKE IT!

STEP 1

LAYER Add the oil to the pan. Layer the onion, garlic, spices, parsley stalks, lemon zest and juice, and chicken thighs, in the pan.

Add just enough water to cover the chicken (about 1¾ cups should be enough depending on the size of the pan), then add the carrots and zucchini. Do not stir.

STEP 2

SIMMER Bring the liquid to a boil over high heat, then turn down the heat to low and cover the pan with a tight-fitting lid (if the fit is loose, use a sheet of foil underneath the lid to make the seal tight). Simmer for 45 minutes.

Stir in the apricots and honey, and season with a little salt to taste.

STEP 3

Turn the heat up a little until the liquid starts to bubble. Cook for another 15 minutes without stirring, with the lid off, until the sauce thickens.

GARNISH Garnish with the reserved parsley leaves and the toasted almonds. This is delicious served with Israeli couscous.

> In Morocco you might sit on floor cushions around a low table. The food is served on platters with everyone helping themselves. Bread is often used to mop up sauces.

THE KEY SPICES

Pepper
The pepper vine grows naturally in south India, and can often be found climbing coconut trees. White pepper is the same as black pepper only riper, with the outer layer removed. Known as "black gold", it was used to pay debts and taxes. In the Middle Ages, pepper was thought to stop you farting!

Cinnamon
Cinnamon is the dried bark of a tree native to southern Asia. It adds a sweet, warming taste to dishes like Moroccan tagines, American pancakes and Swedish buns. Known as the "Spice Coast", India's southern region of Kerala has been a center of spice trade for thousands of years, and is still a major producer and consumer of cinnamon.

Cloves
Cloves are dried, unopened flower buds, which have a very strong taste that numbs your mouth. As well as for cooking, cloves have long been used in medicines, and to keep your breath fresh! Native to the Maluku "Spice Islands" in Indonesia, cloves were one of the first spices to be traded.

Nutmeg
Nutmeg has the bloodiest history of all the spices. The Dutch killed or enslaved the Banda people of the "Spice Islands" in the 1600s and took their nutmeg. When the British won control, they took trees to Grenada in the Caribbean, where it's still grown today. The nutmeg tree produces two spices: nutmeg and mace.

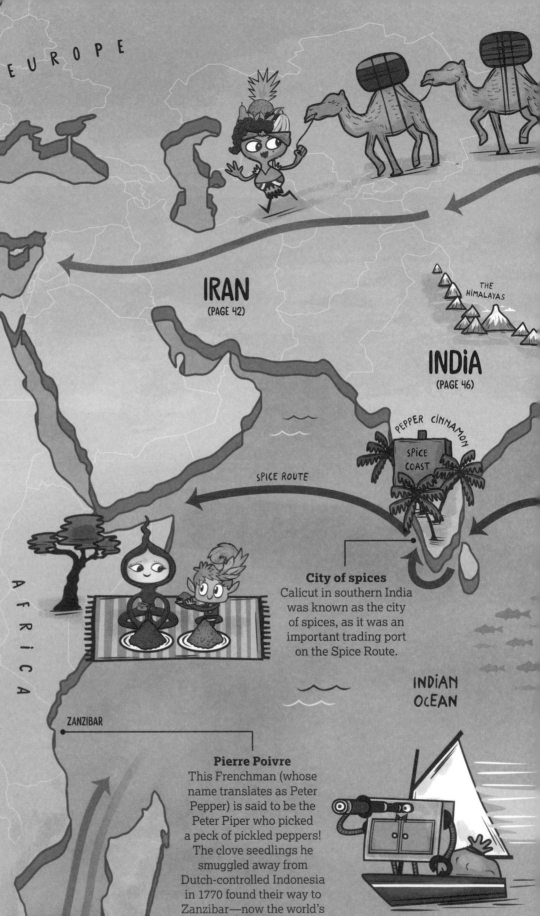

EUROPE

IRAN
(PAGE 42)

THE HIMALAYAS

INDIA
(PAGE 46)

SPICE ROUTE

PEPPER CINNAMON

SPICE COAST

City of spices
Calicut in southern India was known as the city of spices, as it was an important trading port on the Spice Route.

AFRICA

ZANZIBAR

INDIAN OCEAN

Pierre Poivre
This Frenchman (whose name translates as Peter Pepper) is said to be the Peter Piper who picked a peck of pickled peppers! The clove seedlings he smuggled away from Dutch-controlled Indonesia in 1770 found their way to Zanzibar—now the world's largest producer.

Vasco da Gama
This Portuguese sailor's voyage around the southern tip of Africa, in 1497, opened up a new sea route to and from Europe and the "Spice Islands".

ASIA AND AUSTRALIA

The Indian Ocean sits between the continents of Africa, Asia, and Australia. It was used for centuries by ancient civilizations to transport precious riches by boat along a route known as the Spice Route.

Spices were once so valuable that huge empires were built by trading in them, and fierce battles were fought over them. Along with the Silk Road in the north, the Spice Route connected distant cultures in the east and west, and shaped much of the world we know today.

ASIA

SILK ROAD

CHINA
(PAGE 50)

THAILAND
(PAGE 56)

The Silk Road
While spices were mainly shipped by sea, other riches like silk were transported by land through China and the Middle East.

Spice wars
The English and Dutch spent a hundred years fighting over cloves in the Indonesian "Spice Islands".

PACIFIC OCEAN

GRENADA 11,591 MILES

SPICE ISLANDS

INDONESIA

CLOVES   NUTMEG

Island of Spice
Grenada, one of the world's largest producers of nutmeg, is over 11,000 miles from Indonesia where nutmeg was first discovered.

AUSTRALIA
(PAGE 60)

Australian Spices
While the spices of Asia traveled far and wide, becoming popular in kitchens around the world, those from Australia remained relatively unknown. Seeds from native plants like the Wattle bush and Mountain Pepper tree can be dried and used to add unusual spicy flavors to food.

N
W   E
S

Iran

Until 1935, Iran was known as Persia, and "Persian" is still a term used today to describe Iranian cooking. Once a major point on the ancient Silk Road, the region has a rich history stretching back thousands of years. Iranians today are cooking with many of the same ingredients used by their ancestors in 500 BCE.

Persian food often combines sweet and sour flavors, and is beautifully decorated with jewel-like ingredients. It's customary for meals to be laid out on carpets, with diners sitting on cushions around the edge. So join the gang for this sumptuous spread, which is as much a feast for the eyes as it is for the tummy!

Persian timeline

AD 1400
Tomatoes arrived in Persia from the Americas and have become a favorite ingredient today.

AD 800
Some of the earliest windmills, for grinding grain into flour, are thought to have been built in Persia.

AD 700
Cookies are believed to have been invented in Persia. They make a good travel snack as they keep well.

AD 50
Peaches were spreading through Persia to Europe along the Silk Road by this time.

I LOVE NIBBLING ON SABZI BETWEEN COURSES!

I CAN TASTE DILL, CORIANDER, PARSLEY, AND CHIVES...

...AND MINT!

...AND THIS ONE'S COOL IN SUMMER.

Cold yogurt soup
(with ice cubes, cucumbers, and raisins)

Sabzi
(a mixture of fresh herbs)

Warm yogurt soup
(with fresh herbs, spinach, and lentils)

Koofteh
These spicy lamb treats have a hidden prize in the center (often a boiled egg or walnuts). Some think this might have been the beginnings of the Scotch egg!

THIS SOUP IS FAB IN WINTER, LEXI!

THERE'S A PRIZE IN THE KOOFTEH. AWESOME!

Pistachios

Iran is a major grower of pistachios. When the nuts are ready, the shells start to open at one end, revealing the green kernels. Iranians call this "khandan", which means "laughing"!

CHEF'S PERSIAN
JEWELED RiCE & LAMB

SERVES 4

PREPARATION
• Rice: 10 minutes
• Lamb: 5 minutes

COOKING
• Rice: 25 minutes
• Lamb: 25 minutes

ESSENTIAL EQUIPMENT
• Aluminum foil
• Clean dish towel
• Large skillet

RICE
• **unsalted butter (1⅓ tbsp)**
• **easy-cook basmati rice (1⅓ cups)**, *rinsed in a bowl and drained*
• **boiling water (1¾ cups)**
• **¼ tsp saffron** (optional)
• **shelled pistachios (⅔ cup)**
• **dried cranberries (¼ cup)**
• **fresh parsley leaves (⅔ cup)**, *finely chopped*
• **pinch of salt**

LAMB
• **juice of 1 lemon**
• **3 tbsp olive oil**
• **2 tbsp plain yogurt**
• **handful of fresh mint**, *finely chopped*
• **1 large white onion**, *finely chopped*
• **1 tsp ground cinnamon**
• **1 tsp ground cardamom**
• **1 tsp ground cumin**
• **1 tsp ground coriander**
• **grind of black pepper**
• **lean ground lamb (18oz)**
• **1 tbsp tomato paste**

TO SERVE
• **watercress** (or other salad leaves)

> THE JEWEL-LIKE COLORS OF THE INGREDIENTS MAKE MY RiCE LOOK REALLY SPECIAL.

STEP 1

THE RICE

 Melt the butter in a medium-sized saucepan over low heat. Stir in the basmati rice, coating all the grains with butter. Pour in the boiling water, stir, turn up the heat and bring to a boil.

Once the water is bubbling, place a sheet of foil over the pan and then the lid, to make a good seal. Then turn the heat down to low. Cook the rice for 15 minutes. Do not stir or remove the lid. Meanwhile, if using saffron, put it in a bowl with a teaspoon of boiling water.

STEP 2

When the rice is cooked, turn off the heat. If using saffron, put two tablespoons of the rice into the saffron water, mix and cover with the foil from the saucepan.

MIX Place a clean dish towel over the remaining rice in the saucepan and put the lid back on. Leave for 10 minutes. Then tip the white rice into a large bowl, and mix in the yellow saffron rice, pistachios, cranberries, parsley, and a pinch of salt.

STEP 3

THE LAMB

First, make a dressing from the lemon juice, 2 tablespoons of the olive oil, the yogurt, and the mint. Mix well in a bowl and set aside.

Heat the remaining tablespoon of olive oil in a large skillet over medium heat and gently fry the onion for about 8 minutes until soft and slightly brown. Stir in all the dry spices, then add the lamb and fry for another 10 minutes, until cooked through. Stir in the tomato paste, season with salt to taste, and cook for 2 minutes.

 Serve with a drizzle of the dressing over the lamb and a salad of watercress.

India

India is big—from north to south it would cover a distance equal to that from the icy fjords of Norway to the Sahara Desert. At least five major faiths are worshiped, and over 100 languages are spoken.

So it's not surprising that the food eaten across the country is just as diverse. What's grown and eaten in the north of India can be quite different to the south. How many differences can you find?

The tandoor
This is an important item for cooking naan bread, lamb kebabs, and tandoori chicken.

Naan bread

Chicken tikka

Tandoor
(outdoor oven made of clay)

Burns charcoal

The biggest mountain range on Earth!

THE HIMALAYAS

Saffron
The sight of this growing in Jammu and Kashmir is beautiful. More than 1,500 stigmas from crocus flowers have to be picked to make 1 gram of the spice!

Meat
More lamb, mutton, and poultry is eaten in the north of India than in the south, but it's always served in small portions.

SNACKS ARE SOLD AT TRAIN STATIONS THROUGH THE WINDOWS!

Festival of Holi
At this Hindu festival people throw colorful powder and feast on colorful sugar.

KRISHNA, THE HINDU GOD OF LOVE, LIKES DAIRY FOOD

Krishna

TRY CHAI'S NORTH–SOUTH CURRY!

Green chilies (use fresh)

Red chilies (use dried)

Festival of Dussehra
As part of this festival, pumpkins are smashed outside homes for good luck.

Tea
India is the world's second-largest producer of tea (after China). The aromatic drink is made by pouring hot water over the dried leaves of the "Camellia sinensis" bush.

Chilies
Southern cooks use lots of chilies, which are believed to cool the body in the steamy climate by making you sweat! Five hundred years after the Portuguese brought chilies to India, the country is now the world's biggest grower and consumer of them.

TEA PLANTATION

Vegetarianism
There are more vegetarians in southern India. Strict Hindus, Jains, and Taoists don't eat animal products due to their religious beliefs.

Indian bread

This "roti" bread is super-simple to make. Other delicious Indian breads you could try include "poori", "paratha", "naan", "kulcha", and "rumali"—which means "handkerchief"!

CHAI'S INDIAN

NORTH-SOUTH CURRY

SERVES 4

PREPARATION
- Curry:
  10–15 minutes
- Roti: 15 minutes
  (+ 30 minutes
  resting)

COOKING
- Curry: 45 minutes
- Roti: 5 minutes

ESSENTIAL EQUIPMENT
- Large saucepan
  with a lid
- Mortar and pestle
  (or you can use
  a food processor)
- Rolling pin (for roti)

ROTI
- **wholemeal flour (9 tbsp)**
- **all-purpose flour (9 tbsp)**
- **pinch of salt**
- **water (scant ½ cup)**

PASTE
- **4 cloves of garlic,** *peeled and roughly chopped*
- **fresh ginger (⅓ cup),** *peeled and roughly chopped*
- **2 tsp ground turmeric**
- **½ tsp chili powder**
- **1 tsp ground cumin**
- **1 tsp ground coriander**
- **3 tbsp white wine vinegar**

CURRY
- **1 tbsp vegetable oil**
- **1 large white onion**, *peeled and finely chopped*
- **8 chicken thighs (approx. 1¼lb)**, (free range or organic if possible) *skinless and boneless, cut in half*
- **fresh tomatoes (1¼lb)**, *roughly chopped*

TO SERVE
- **a handful of fresh cilantro leaves,** *finely chopped*
- **basmati rice**
- **natural yogurt**

STEP 1

Mix both types of flour in a large bowl with a pinch of salt, then make a well in the center. Slowly add the water to the well, mixing in the flour as you go. Stop adding water when the dough becomes slightly sticky.

KNEAD Transfer the dough to a clean, floured work surface, and knead it for 10 minutes until it becomes elastic in texture. Return it to the bowl, cover with a clean, damp dish towel and leave somewhere warm for 30 minutes.

YOU CAN USE MY PASTE AS A STARTING POINT FOR MAKING OTHER CURRIES. ADD COCONUT FOR A KORMA, GREEN CHILIES FOR A JALFREZI, AND PAPRIKA FOR A ROGAN JOSH.

STEP 2

SNIFF Crush all the paste ingredients in a mortar and pestle (or whiz in a food processor) until they are smooth and completely combined. (Be sure to have a sniff while you do it!)

Heat the vegetable oil in a large saucepan over medium-low heat. Add the onion and sweat until it is soft but not brown (about 8–10 minutes), stirring regularly to prevent it sticking. Add the paste and continue stirring for another 2–3 minutes.

Add the chicken to the pan and fry for 4–5 minutes, stirring continuously, until the meat is sealed (has turned white) all over. Mix in the tomatoes. Put the lid on the pan and turn the heat down low. Simmer for 20 minutes, stirring every 5 minutes or so.

STEP 3

ROLL Meanwhile, divide the dough into four balls. On a clean, floured work surface roll out each ball into a small disc. They should be about 6 inches in diameter and ⅛ inch thick.

Heat a large nonstick skillet over high heat until hot, then turn down to medium heat. Add a roti to the pan and cook it until bubbles appear (about 20–25 seconds), before turning and cooking the other side in the same way. The roti should change color, with darker patches where the bubbles touched the pan. Repeat with the other three roti.

By now the curry should be nearly ready. Taste and add a little salt if needed. Increase the heat to medium and cook for another 5 minutes, or until the sauce has thickened.

Garnish with a sprinkling of chopped fresh cilantro leaves, and serve with boiled basmati rice and a dollop of plain yogurt.

CHINA
IN THE KITCHEN

China is a huge country with a long history. The ancient Chinese introduced many great inventions to the world, including fireworks, paper, printing... and noodles, the earliest known form of pasta!

A quick look around a typical Chinese kitchen reveals a whole host of interesting utensils, cooking vessels, and eating implements (not to mention ingredients). How many do you recognize?

ESSENTIAL IMPLEMENTS

Cleavers

Chopsticks
Unless you're eating soup, or slippery things like tofu, these are what you eat with in China.

Chopping is the first skill to be mastered in the Chinese kitchen, and there are lots of different types of cutting to learn...

Ding
(cubes)

Tiao
(strips)

Mi li
(rice grains)

Ma'er duo
(horse ears)

Zhi jia pian
(thumbnail slices)

Si
(slivers)

Steamer
Used in Chinese cookery since the Stone Age. Steamed fish, crabs, and dumplings are all popular dishes.

Steamed food is very healthy, as vitamins are kept that would be destroyed in boiling water.

Each basket contains a different part of the meal.

Steam rises up to cook the contents.

KEY INGREDIENTS

Ginger
The Chinese make lots of medicines using this warm, spicy root. Scrambled eggs with ginger is thought to stop a cough.

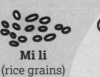

Chilies
They're finely chopped and sprinkled in stir-fries, or made into a paste for spicy Sichuan and Hunan dishes.

Scallions
Milder than big onions. The word "onion" comes from the Latin word "unio" which means "large pearl".

Soybeans
Soybeans are an excellent substitute for meat due to their high protein content. They're used to make soy sauce, tofu, and even milk!

Garlic
Rich in vitamin B, which helps you to feel happy.

Five spice
A blend of star anise, fennel seeds, cloves, cinnamon, and Sichuan peppercorns. It tastes sweet, hot, fragrant, salty, and pungent all at once!

CHINA
SAMPLING STREET FOOD

A trip to a night market in China is an adventure. It's busy, noisy and full of life! "Xiaochi" are small snacks that can be bought and eaten on the street at any time of day or night in China. It's an opportunity to taste regional specialties from far and wide.

With so many unusual and tasty snacks to choose from, which would you like to try?

Entomophagy (insects as food)
By 2050, there will be twice as many people in the world to feed. Could eating insects be the answer? Farming insects releases less greenhouse gas into the atmosphere than raising livestock, so is better for the environment. In China, it's common to find insects being served as a crunchy snack in street markets.

Locust
Easy to harvest as they are found in swarms

Silkworm

Mealworm
Tastes like nutty shrimp

What is "dan dan"?

The name "dan dan" means
a carrying pole that was used
by people who walked the
streets in China, selling food
to passers-by. The pole was
carried over the shoulder,
with a basket at each end.
One contained the noodles,
and the other held the sauce.

BENTLEY'S CHINESE
DAN DAN NOODLES

SERVES 4

PREPARATION
10 minutes

COOKING
10 minutes

ESSENTIAL EQUIPMENT
• Wok

BROTH
• **1 vegetable bouillon cube**
  dissolved in 1 quart of boiling water
• **egg noodles (about 8½oz)**

STIR-FRY
• **1 tbsp peanut oil**
  (or sunflower oil)
• **ground pork (9oz)**
  (free range or organic if possible)
• **2 tsp Sichuan peppercorns**
  (also called Szechuan and Szechwan)
  crushed in a mortar and pestle
• **3 tbsp rice vinegar**
• **3 tbsp light soy sauce**
• **4 scallions**, *trimmed and sliced*
• **spinach (about 7oz)**

TO SERVE
• **½ fresh red chile** (optional),
  seeded and chopped

SICHUAN PEPPERCORNS CAN MAKE YOUR MOUTH FEEL STRANGELY NUMB!

STEP 1

Heat the vegetable bouillon in a saucepan and leave to simmer.

STIR-FRY Heat the oil in a wok over high heat, then add the ground pork and Sichuan peppercorns. Stir-fry for 3 minutes until the pork is cooked through.

SMELL Add the rice vinegar, soy sauce, and scallions, and stir-fry for another minute. Turn off the heat and stir in the spinach so it wilts, and is mixed in with the pork. Then set aside.

STEP 2

Add the noodles to the bouillon and simmer until they are cooked.

In 2002, archaeologists in China found a bowl containing the world's oldest-known noodles. They were about 4,000 years old!

STEP 3

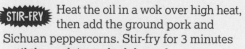
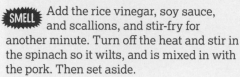

GARNISH Strain the noodle stock through a sieve into the wok, then share the cooked noodles between four bowls.

Stir the noodle stock in with the pork mixture and add an equal amount to each bowl.

If you want to add a little extra heat, garnish with some chopped red chile.

Thailand

Thailand is a mainly Buddhist country in Southeast Asia. Thai cooking beautifully combines five key tastes—sour, fragrant, salty, hot, and sweet.

The Ingreedies are having fun on a floating market, and it looks like some interesting Thai flavor explosions are happening!

Tamarind
The tamarind tree has pods that contain very small beans surrounded by a sour-tasting pulp. Thais eat this pulp with a sprinkling of sugar, or mix it with water to make a sour juice.

ARGHH!!!

SOUR!

Lime juice
Limes add a fresh, zingy flavor to Thai cooking.

Pickles
Carrots, cucumbers, mushrooms, ginger, and stink beans are all kept in jars with vinegar.

WHOOPS! LOOK OUT, LEXI!

Lemongrass
When you crush the stalks of this grass, a lemony smell and taste is released. It's delicious in curries and herbal teas.

Holy basil
This herb has a clove-like fragrance. Basil seeds swell when they're soaked in water and in Thailand are used in a jelly.

Cilantro leaf
Thais scatter this highly scented herb over everything (or mash up its roots for curry pastes).

FRAGRANT!

Kaffir lime leaves
The smell of this plant is so delicious it's also used in perfume and shampoo. Its leaves have a figure-eight shape.

SALTY!

Fish sauce
Add a drop or two to your curry, or use it to make a dipping sauce.

Shrimp paste
Adds a delicious salty taste to your curry paste.

FISH SAUCE, ANYONE?

FLOATING MARKETS
For centuries in Thailand, long before the construction of major roads and railways, food was transported by water. This led to the rise of floating markets, where food was bought and sold on boats. Nowadays, they're a bustling hub of activity, also visited by tourists looking to sample a slice of Thailand's rich history.

I THINK WE'RE GOING TO GET WET!

Mouse-dropping chilies
These tiny, super-hot chilies are grown in gardens all over Thailand, and can be green or red.

HOT!

Nam Prik sauce
You'll find this on every table at every meal. It's made from dried red chilies, lime juice, Thai fish sauce, garlic, and sugar.

THIS GIVES ME AN IDEA FOR A RECIPE...

Coconut milk
The coconut is one of the most useful fruits in the world. You can eat it, drink its water, make bowls out of its shell, cook with its oil, and make clothes from its fibers. Coconut milk is made by pouring boiling water over grated coconut, and then squeezing the liquid.

Palm sugar
This is made from the sap of a type of palm tree. Cuts are made in the tree trunk and the sticky sap flows out. The sugar is brown and crumbly.

Mango
This fruit is eaten ripe with sticky rice, or unripe (green), dipped in salt and dried chile.

SWEET!

CHECK OUT LEXI'S TASTY RAINBOW VEGETABLES!

Fresh fast food

Thai dishes are mostly made of fresh ingredients (rather than powdered or dried), cooked quickly in a wok. As a result, the food tastes just as bright and vibrant as it looks, and nearly always has a delicious crunch to it.

"Sanùk" is Thai for "fun", something that would certainly describe this cheerful cuisine!

RAINBOW VEGETABLES

SERVES 4

PREPARATION
25 minutes

COOKING
10 minutes

ESSENTIAL EQUIPMENT
• Wok
• Mortar and pestle (or you can use a food processor)

PASTE
• **3 large cloves of garlic**, *peeled and crushed*
• **ginger (⅓ cup)**, *peeled and finely chopped*
• **1 large red chile**, *seeded and finely chopped*
• **3 small shallots**, *peeled and finely chopped*
• **½ tsp tamarind paste**
• **3 tsp lemongrass paste** (or 1½ sticks of fresh lemongrass)
• **1½ tsp tomato paste**

STIR-FRY
• **1 tbsp peanut or sunflower oil**
• **mixed crunchy vegetables (21oz)** (such as baby corn, snow peas, red pepper, broccoli rabe, green beans, sugar snap peas and carrots), *chopped into bite-sized pieces*
• **coconut milk (1¾ cups)**
• **2 tsp fish sauce**
• **juice of 1 lime**
• **4 scallions**, *trimmed and chopped*
• **soft, ribbon, straight-to-wok noodles (21oz)**

TO SERVE
• **small bunch of fresh cilantro**, *leaves roughly chopped*
• **salted peanuts (¾ cup)** (optional)
• **wedges of lime** (optional)
• **1 fresh red chile**, *seeded and finely chopped* (optional)

> ONCE YOUR PASTE IS MASHED AND YOUR VEGGIES ARE CHOPPED, MY CRUNCHY STIR-FRY COOKS SUPER-FAST!

STEP 1

CRUSH Crush all the ingredients for the paste in a mortar and pestle (more satisfying) or blitz them in a food processor (easier). You should have a fairly smooth, well-mixed paste that smells delicious.

STEP 2

Make sure all the rest of your ingredients are prepared (chopped and juiced) including your garnishes. Once you start cooking, the stir-fry will be ready very quickly.

STIR-FRY Heat the oil in a large wok until hot. Add your paste and stir-fry for 1 minute. Add the mixed crunchy vegetables and stir-fry for 2 minutes.

STEP 3

Add the coconut milk, fish sauce, lime juice, and scallions, bring to a boil and cook for 4 minutes.

Add the noodles, mix well so the noodles are all separated and combined with the sauce, and cook for a final 2 minutes.

SPRINKLE Serve with a sprinkling of the fresh cilantro leaves. The other garnishes are best served in little bowls so people can help themselves.

AUSTRALIA

As we reach the end of our journey, what better way to celebrate than with friends and food? Australian life is all about the great outdoors, and there's plenty of fun to be had finding your dinner.

So light the barbecue and relax, as the sun starts to set on our adventure around the world.

A-hunting we will go
Early Aborigines, Australia's native people, ate green ants and made kangaroo tail soup. They also hunted wallaby, goanna, crocodile, and emu.

IF I'D KNOWN YOU WERE COMING, I'D HAVE BAKED A SNAKE...

BAKED A SNAKE, BAKED A SNAKE...

Sing a campfire song
There's an Australian version of an old song that refers to baking snake (which tastes a bit like chicken).

THAT DAMPER BREAD LOOKS TASTY!

ER, CHEF... WILL THIS FIT ON THE BARBIE?

Broadbill swordfish

Make damper bread
Stockmen traveled around remote areas of Australia for months, looking after their livestock. Carrying just flour, sugar, and tea, they baked damper bread made from basic dough in the ashes of their campfires.

Go fishing
Most Australians live close to the coast, so super-fresh seafood is a major part of their diet.

Squid

King George whiting

Bream

Calamari

Balmain bug
A type of lobster, lovely in a lemony, herby salad.

Tropical rock lobster
Often caught with a spear. Great barbecued with lemongrass.

Octopus

Find some bush tucker
With more than 350 edible native plants in the Australian bush (or countryside), nature provides an amazing array of nuts, berries, and fruit to feast on. Tuck in!

Lilly pilly
Like cranberries. Makes great jam.

Wattleseed
Tastes like chocolate, coffee, and hazelnut. Yum!

Kakadu plums
One of the world's best sources of Vitamin C.

Macadamia nuts
The shells are so hard they will break your nutcracker!

Bunya nut
Aboriginal people traditionally held special festivals to feast on these kernels.

Finger lime
A burst of tasty tanginess.

THE PERFECT END TO OUR JOURNEY!

BE BRAVE, LEXI. BE BRAVE!

Be brave
Witchetty grubs are nutty-tasting moth larvae. They're good raw, but don't eat the head!

ANYONE FANCY A FAREWELL FUSION BURGER?

HEY! HANDS OFF MY BURGER!

CHUCK ANOTHER SHRIMP ON THE BARBIE, CHEF!

tea

billycan

Have a barbie!
Australians love to barbecue—they even have a barbie on Christmas Day! They look forward to the weekend when friends and family share chops, steaks, fish, shrimp, and sausages cooked over hot coals.

Blue swimmer crab
They hide in the sand and pounce on prey.

Banana shrimp

Tiger shrimp

Sea urchin
Tastes salty and sweet with a creamy texture.

Greenlip abalone
Eat them raw!

Southern saucer scallop
Delicious with chile and lime butter.

Shrimp are related to crabs and lobsters, and are a favorite food here and around the world.

Jumbo shrimp

61

Fruit salad

Mango and papaya trees love Australia's warm climate. Their fruit is perfect for putting in a summertime salad.

What is "fusion" food?

Modern Australian food mixes flavors from around the world with local ingredients. Many Greeks and Italians came to live in the country, followed by people from Vietnam, Korea, and Thailand. They brought flavors from home, and mixed them with the ingredients and recipes of traditional Australia to create fusion food.

CHEF'S AUSTRALIAN
FUSION BURGERS

SERVES 4

PREPARATION
• Burgers:
  10 minutes
  (+ 1 hour resting)
• Salad: 5 minutes

COOKING
15–20 minutes

BURGERS
• **4 small shallots**, *skinned and very finely chopped*
• **1 large clove garlic**, *peeled and crushed*
• **1 red chile** (optional), *seeded and very finely chopped*
• **zest of 1 lime**
• **handful of fresh cilantro leaves**, *very finely chopped*
• **1 tbsp soy sauce**
• **15% fat ground beef (18oz)**
• **1 tbsp olive oil**
• **4 brioche buns**

QUICK FUSION KETCHUP
• **2 tbsp tomato ketchup**
• **1 tbsp soy sauce**
• **juice of 1 lime**
• **1 scallion**, *finely chopped*
• **handful of fresh cilantro leaves**, *finely chopped*

SALAD
• **1 small bag of salad leaves (approx. 3oz)**
• **cashews (scant ½ cup)**
• **1 mango**, *peeled and cut into small chunks*
• **1 tbsp balsamic vinegar**
• **2 tbsp olive oil**
• **1 tsp wholegrain mustard**

> MY RECIPE FUSES THE FLAVORS OF THAILAND WITH THE FAMOUS AUSSIE MEAL —THE BARBECUE!

STEP 1

BURGERS

MIX Place all the burger ingredients except the beef and the olive oil (and buns!) in a bowl and mix well. Add the beef and combine, but be careful not to overwork the mixture.

Make 4 balls from the mixture and place them on a sheet of waxed paper. Leave them to chill in the fridge for 1 hour.

Meanwhile, combine all the ketchup ingredients in a bowl and set aside.

STEP 2

MANGO AND CASHEW SALAD

TOAST Toast the cashews for 1–2 minutes in a dry skillet over medium heat until they start to turn slightly darker.

For the dressing, mix the balsamic vinegar, olive oil, and mustard in a small cup.

POUR Just before you're ready to eat, assemble the salad leaves, toasted cashews, and mango in a bowl. Then pour over the dressing (doing this at the last minute keeps your leaves nice and crispy).

STEP 3

Heat the olive oil in a skillet and add the burgers. Gently press down each one to flatten slightly. Cook for 7–8 minutes without moving them. Then flip them, and fry for another 7–8 minutes until they are cooked through.

Halve the brioche buns and lightly toast the insides. Serve the burgers in the buns with a dollop of your ketchup, and a serving of salad.

Great on the barbecue too!

About Ingreedies

Ingreedies was dreamed up by designers Zoë Bather and Joe Sharpe, and illustrator Chris Dickason. They're passionate about food, and believe it has the power to educate children about the world around them. Through knowledge, stories, and activities, they want to get kids excited about the meals they eat, with the help of their band of intrepid food explorers—The Ingreedies.

www.ingreedies.com

LAURENCE KING

Published in 2016 by
Laurence King Publishing Ltd
361–373 City Road
London EC1V 1LR
United Kingdom

Tel: 020 7841 6900
Fax: 020 7841 6977
email: enquiries@laurenceking.com
www.laurenceking.com

A catalog record for this book is available from the British Library.

ISBN: 978-1-78067-830-6

Printed in China

Written by Zoë Bather & Joe Sharpe
Illustrated by Chris Dickason

Design: Zoë Bather & Joe Sharpe
Photography: Simon Pask
Additional typography: Kim Cowie & Peter Keech
Americanizer: Lee Faber

THANK YOU

Ingreedies exists because of two people—Lottie and Tia. Thank you for eating our recipes and proving it works!

Thank you to our families—Nick, Mary, Naomi, and Chris; Brian, Helen, Hannah, and Roch; Stuart, Lynda, Daniela, Kara, and Philip—for nurturing and sharing our love of food.

Special thanks to all our loyal recipe testers—Maria, Tom, Finn, and Morwenna; Nic, Richard, Tom, and Lucy; Holly, Richard, and Frida; Yvette and Stuart; Helen and Brian; Nick and Mary; Kim and Chris; Nay and Mike; Pete, Teresa, Etta, Patrick, and Hannah; Paul, Sarah, Natalia, and Tabitha; Bryony and Tom; Panja, Paul-Mark, Isaac, and Lois; and Amy and Sam of Freshly Ground PR, along with their niece Jessica—without you we'd only have half a book!

Thank you to Laurence King, our fantastic publisher; and Elizabeth Jenner and Melissa Danny for their editorial wisdom, and guiding us through our first book. A big thank you to Kim Cowie and Peter Keech for their beautiful custom typography and ongoing support; and photographer Simon Pask, for helping make our dishes look delicious.

Thank you to Made in Me for giving us our first platform, and to Applied Works for the ongoing help and space (both time and physical) that has made Ingreedies possible.

Lastly, to Eric Huang, for your unending support and belief in Ingreedies from the very beginning—we salute you!

Zoë, Joe, and Chris

SWEDEN

THE BRITISH ISLES

FRANCE

ITALY

MOROCCO

USA

MEXICO

BRAZIL